WITHDRAWN

Owls
and
Pussy-cats

ILLUSTRATED BY NICKI PALIN

Owls
and
Pussy-cats

NONSENSE VERSE
by Edward Lear and Lewis Carroll

PETER BEDRICK BOOKS

NEW YORK

First American edition published by
Peter Bedrick Books
2112 Broadway
New York, NY 10023

Published by agreement with Oxford University Press, Oxford, England

Library of Congress Cataloging-in-Publication Data
Carroll, Lewis, 1832–1898.
Owls and Pussycats: nonsense verse / by Lewis Carroll and Edward
Lear: illustrated by Nicki Palin. — 1st American ed.
Includes index.
Summary: An illustrated collection of nonsense verse by Lewis Carroll
and Edward Lear, including "The Mock Turtle's Song," "Jabberwocky,"
"The Jumblies," and "The Dong with a Luminous Nose."
ISBN 0-87226-366-5 (acid-free paper)
1. Children's poetry, English. 2. Nonsense verses, English. [1. English
poetry—Collections. 2. Nonsense verses.] I. Lear, Edward, 1812–1888.
II. Palin, Nicki. 111. Ill. Title. PR4611.A4 1993

Typeset by Pentacor PLC, High Wycombe, Bucks
Printed in Hong Kong
on acid-free paper

Contents

Self-Portrait of the Laureate of Nonsense

How pleasant to know Mr Lear!
  Who has written such volumes of stuff!
Some think him ill-tempered and queer,
  But a few think him pleasant enough.

E.L.

Dedication from Through the Looking-glass

Child of the pure unclouded brow
  And dreaming eyes of wonder!
Though time be fleet, and I and thou
  Are half a life asunder,
Thy loving smile will surely hail
The love-gift of a fairy-tale.

L.C.

Jabberwocky

———

'Twas brillig, and the slithy toves
　Did gyre and gimble in the wabe;
All mimsy were the borogoves,
　　And the mome raths outgrabe.

'Beware the Jabberwock, my son!
　The jaws that bite, the claws that catch!
Beware the Jubjub bird, and shun
　　The frumious Bandersnatch!'

He took his vorpal sword in hand:
　Long time the manxome foe he sought –
So rested he by the Tumtum tree,
　　And stood awhile in thought.

And as in uffish thought he stood,
    The Jabberwock, with eyes of flame,
Came whiffling through the tulgey wood,
    And burbled as it came!

One, two! One, two! And through and through
    The vorpal blade went snicker-snack!
He left it dead, and with its head
    He went galumphing back.

'And hast thou slain the Jabberwock?
    Come to my arms, my beamish boy!
O frabjous day! Callooh! Callay!'
    He chortled in his joy.

'Twas brillig, and the slithy toves
    Did gyre and gimble in the wabe;
All mimsy were the borogoves,
    And the mome raths outgrabe.

                                    L.C.

How Doth the
Little Crocodile

How doth the little crocodile
  Improve his shining tail,
And pour the waters of the Nile
  On every golden scale!

How cheerfully he seems to grin,
  How neatly spreads his claws,
And welcomes little fishes in
  With gently smiling jaws!

L.C.

The Jumblies

———

I

They went to sea in a Sieve, they did,
  In a Sieve they went to sea:
In spite of all their friends could say,
On a winter's morn, on a stormy day,
  In a Sieve they went to sea!
And when the Sieve turned round and round,
And every one cried, 'You'll all be drowned!'
They called aloud, 'Our Sieve ain't big,
But we don't care a button! we don't care a fig!
  In a Sieve we'll go to sea!'
    Far and few, far and few,
      Are the lands where the Jumblies live;
      Their heads are green, and their hands are blue,
      And they went to sea in a Sieve.

II

They sailed away in a Sieve, they did,
  In a Sieve they sailed so fast,
With only a beautiful pea-green veil
Tied with a riband by way of a sail,
  To a small tobacco-pipe mast;
And every one said, who saw them go,
'O won't they be soon upset, you know!
For the sky is dark, and the voyage is long,
And happen what may, it's extremely wrong
  In a Sieve to sail so fast!'
    Far and few, far and few,
      Are the lands where the Jumblies live;
      Their heads are green, and their hands are blue,
      And they went to sea in a Sieve.

III

The water it soon came in, it did,
    The water it soon came in;
So to keep them dry, they wrapped their feet
In a pinky paper all folded neat,
    And they fastened it down with a pin.
And they passed the night in a crockery-jar,
And each of them said, 'How wise we are!
Though the sky be dark, and the voyage be long,
Yet we never can think we were rash or wrong,
    While round in our Sieve we spin!'
      Far and few, far and few,
        Are the lands where the Jumblies live;
        Their heads are green, and their hands are blue,
        And they went to sea in a Sieve.

IV

And all night long they sailed away;
    And when the sun went down,
They whistled and warbled a moony song
To the echoing sound of a coppery gong,
    In the shade of the mountains brown.
'O Timballo! How happy we are,
When we live in a sieve and a crockery-jar
And all night long in the moonlight pale,
We sail away with a pea-green sail,
    In the shade of the mountains brown!'
    Far and few, far and few,
        Are the lands where the Jumblies live;
        Their heads are green, and their hands are blue,
        And they went to sea in a Sieve.

V

They sailed to the Western Sea, they did,
   To a land all covered with trees,
And they bought an Owl, and a useful Cart,
And a pound of Rice, and a Cranberry Tart,
   And a hive of silvery Bees.
And they bought a Pig, and some green Jack-daws,
And a lovely Monkey with lollipop paws,
And forty bottles of Ring-Bo-Ree,
   And no end of Stilton Cheese.
     Far and few, far and few,
       Are the lands where the Jumblies live;
      Their heads are green, and their hands are blue,
       And they went to sea in a Sieve.

VI

And in twenty years they all came back,
    In twenty years or more,
And every one said, 'How tall they've grown!
For they've been to the Lakes, and the Torrible Zone,
    And the hills of the Chankly Bore';
And they drank their health, and gave them a feast
Of dumplings made of beautiful yeast;
And every one said, 'If we only live,
We too will go to sea in a Sieve, –
    To the hills of the Chankly Bore!'
      Far and few, far and few,
        Are the lands where the Jumblies live;
      Their heads are green, and their hands are blue,
        And they went to sea in a Sieve.

                              E.L.

The Owl and the Pussy-cat

I

The Owl and the Pussy-cat went to sea
    In a beautiful pea-green boat,
They took some honey, and plenty of money,
    Wrapped up in a five-pound note.
The Owl looked up to the stars above,
    And sang to a small guitar,
'O lovely Pussy! O Pussy, my love,
        What a beautiful Pussy you are
                You are,
                You are!
What a beautiful Pussy you are!'

II

Pussy said to the Owl, 'You elegant fowl!
  How charmingly sweet you sing!
O let us be married! too long we have tarried:
  But what shall we do for a ring?'
They sailed away, for a year and a day,
  To the land where the Bong-tree grows
And there in a wood a Piggy-wig stood
  With a ring at the end of his nose,
        His nose,
        His nose,
  With a ring at the end of his nose.

III

'Dear Pig, are you willing to sell for one shilling
  Your ring?' Said the Piggy, 'I will.'
So they took it away, and were married next day
  By the Turkey who lives on the hill.
They dined on mince, and slices of quince,
  Which they ate with a runcible spoon;
And hand in hand, on the edge of the sand,
  They danced by the light of the moon,
        The moon,
        The moon,
  They danced by the light of the moon.

                                              E.L.

The New Vestments

There lived an old man in the Kingdom of Tess,
Who invented a purely original dress;
And when it was perfectly made and complete,
He opened the door, and walked into the street.

By way of a hat, he'd a loaf of Brown Bread,
In the middle of which he inserted his head; –
His Shirt was made up of no end of dead Mice,
The warmth of whose skins was quite fluffy and nice; –
His Drawers were of Rabbit-skins; – so were his Shoes; –
His Stockings were skins, – but it is not known whose; –
His Waistcoat and Trousers were made of Pork Chops; –
His Buttons were Jujubes, and Chocolate Drops; –
His Coat was all Pancakes with Jam for a border,

And a girdle of Biscuits to keep it in order;
And he wore over all, as a screen from bad weather,
A Cloak of green Cabbage-leaves stitched all together.

He had walked a short way, when he heard a great noise,
Of all sorts of Beasticles, Birdlings, and Boys; –
And from every long street and dark lane in the town
Beasts, Birdles, and Boys in a tumult rushed down.
Two Cows and a half ate his Cabbage-leaf Cloak; –
Four Apes seized his Girdle, which vanished like smoke; –
Three Kids ate up half of his Pancaky Coat, –
And the tails were devour'd by an ancient He-Goat; –
An army of Dogs in a twinkling tore *up* his
Pork Waistcoat and Trousers to give to their Puppies; –
And while they were growling, and mumbling the Chops,
Ten Boys prigged the Jujubes and Chocolate Drops. –
He tried to run back to his house, but in vain,
For Scores of fat Pigs came again and again; –
They rushed out of stables and hovels and doors, –
They tore off his stockings, his shoes, and his drawers; –
And now from the housetops with screechings descend,
Striped, spotted, white, black, and grey Cats without end,
They jumped on his shoulders and knocked off his hat, –
When Crows, Ducks, and Hens made a mincemeat of that; –
They speedily flew at his sleeves in a trice,
And utterly tore up his Shirt of dead Mice; –
They swallowed the last of his Shirt with a squall, –
Whereon he ran home with no clothes on at all.

And he said to himself as he bolted the door,
'I will not wear a similar dress any more,
Any more, any more, any more, never more!'

E.L.

The Walrus and the Carpenter

The sun was shining on the sea,
  Shining with all his might:
He did his very best to make
  The billows smooth and bright –
And this was odd, because it was
  The middle of the night.

The moon was shining sulkily,
  Because she thought the sun
Had got no business to be there
  After the day was done –
'It's very rude of him,' she said,
  'To come and spoil the fun!'

The sea was wet as wet could be,
  The sands were dry as dry.
You could not see a cloud, because
  No cloud was in the sky:
No birds were flying overhead –
  There were no birds to fly.

The Walrus and the Carpenter
  Were walking close at hand;
They wept like anything to see
  Such quantities of sand:
'If this were only cleared away,'
  They said, 'it *would* be grand!'

'If seven maids with seven mops
  Swept it for half a year,
Do you suppose,' the Walrus said,
  'That they could get it clear?'
'I doubt it,' said the Carpenter,
  And shed a bitter tear.

'O Oysters, come and walk with us!'
  The Walrus did beseech.
'A pleasant walk, a pleasant talk,
  Along the briny beach:
We cannot do with more than four,
  To give a hand to each.'

The eldest Oyster looked at him,
    But never a word he said:
The eldest Oyster winked his eye,
    And shook his heavy head –
Meaning to say he did not choose
    To leave the oyster-bed.

But four young Oysters hurried up,
    All eager for the treat:
Their coats were brushed, their faces washed
    Their shoes were clean and neat –
And this was odd, because, you know,
    They hadn't any feet.

Four other Oysters followed them,
    And yet another four;
And thick and fast they came at last,
    And more, and more, and more –
All hopping through the frothy waves,
    And scrambling to the shore.

The Walrus and the Carpenter
   Walked on a mile or so,
And then they rested on a rock
   Conveniently low:
And all the little Oysters stood
   And waited in a row.

'The time has come,' the Walrus said,
   'To talk of many things:
Of shoes – and ships – and sealing-wax –
   Of cabbages – and kings –
And why the sea is boiling hot –
   And whether pigs have wings.'

'But wait a bit,' the Oysters cried,
   'Before we have our chat;
For some of us are out of breath,
   And all of us are fat!'
'No hurry!' said the Carpenter.
   They thanked him much for that.

'A loaf of bread,' the Walrus said,
    'Is what we chiefly need:
Pepper and vinegar besides
    Are very good indeed –
Now if you're ready, Oysters dear,
    We can begin to feed.'

'But not on us!' the Oysters cried,
    Turning a little blue.
'After such kindness, that would be
    A dismal thing to do!'
'The night is fine,' the Walrus said.
    'Do you admire the view?

'It was so kind of you to come!
    And you are very nice!'
The Carpenter said nothing but
    'Cut us another slice:
I wish you were not quite so deaf –
    I've had to ask you twice!'

'It seems a shame,' the Walrus said,
    'To play them such a trick,
After we've brought them out so far,
    And made them trot so quick!'
The Carpenter said nothing but
    'The butter's spread too thick!'

'I weep for you,' the Walrus said:
    'I deeply sympathize.'
With sobs and tears he sorted out
    Those of the largest size,
Holding his pocket-handkerchief
    Before his streaming eyes.

'O Oysters,' said the Carpenter,
    'You've had a pleasant run!
Shall we be trotting home again?'
    But answer came there none –
And this was scarcely odd, because
    They'd eaten every one.

                    L.C.

Evidence Read at the Trial of the Knave of Hearts

They told me you had been to her,
    And mentioned me to him:
She gave me a good character,
    But said I could not swim.

He sent them word I had not gone,
    (We know it to be true):
If she should push the matter on,
    What would become of you?

I gave her one, they gave him two,
    You gave us three or more;
They all returned from him to you,
    Though they were mine before.

If I or she should chance to be
  Involved in this affair,
He trusts to you to set them free,
  Exactly as we were.

My notion was that you had been
  (Before she had this fit)
An obstacle that came between
  Him, and ourselves, and it.

Don't let him know she liked them best,
  For this must ever be
A secret kept from all the rest,
  Between yourself and me.

                                    L.C.

The Pobble who has no Toes

The Pobble who has no toes
   Had once as many as we;
When they said, 'Some day you may lose them all;' –
   He replied, – 'Fish fiddle de-dee!'
And his Aunt Jobiska made him drink,
Lavender water tinged with pink,
For she said, 'The World in general knows
There's nothing so good for a Pobble's toes!'

The Pobble who has no toes,
   Swam across the Bristol Channel;
But before he set out he wrapped his nose,
   In a piece of scarlet flannel.
For his Aunt Jobiska said, 'No harm
Can come to his toes if his nose is warm;
And it's perfectly known that a Pobble's toes
Are safe, – provided he minds his nose.'

The Pobble swam fast and well
    And when boats or ships came near him
He tinkledy-binkledy-winkled a bell
    So that all the world could hear him,
And all the Sailors and Admirals cried,
When they saw him nearing the further side, –
'He has gone to fish, for his Aunt Jobiska's
Runcible Cat with crimson whiskers!'

But before he touched the shore,
    The shore of the Bristol Channel,
A sea-green Porpoise carried away
    His wrapper of scarlet flannel.
And when he came to observe his feet
Formerly garnished with toes so neat
His face at once became forlorn
On perceiving that all his toes were gone!

And nobody ever knew
    From that dark day to the present,
Whoso had taken the Pobble's toes,
    In a manner so far from pleasant.
Whether the shrimps or crawfish grey,
Or crafty Mermaids stole them away –
Nobody knew; and nobody knows
How the Pobble was robbed of his twice five toes!

The Pobble who has no toes
    Was placed in a friendly Bark,
And they rowed him back, and carried him up,
    To his Aunt Jobiska's Park.
And she made him a feast at his earnest wish
Of eggs and buttercups fried with fish; –
And she said, – 'It's a fact the whole world knows,
That Pobbles are happier without their toes.'

E.L.

The Mock Turtle's Song

————

'Will you walk a little faster?' said a whiting to a snail.
'There's a porpoise close behind us, and he's treading on my tail.
See how eagerly the lobsters and the turtles all advance!
They are waiting on the shingle – will you come and join the dance?
  Will you, won't you, will you, won't you, will you join the dance?
  Will you, won't you, will you, won't you, won't you join the dance?'

'You can really have no notion how delightful it will be,
When they take us up and throw us, with the lobsters, out to sea!'
But the snail replied 'Too far, too far!' and gave a look askance –
Said he thanked the whiting kindly, but he would not join the dance.
    Would not, could not, would not, could not, would not join the dance.
    Would not, could not, would not, could not, could not join the dance.

'What matter's it how far we go?' his scaly friend replied.
'There is another shore, you know, upon the other side.
The further off from England the nearer is to France –
Then turn not pale, beloved snail, but come and join the dance.
    Will you, won't you, will you, won't you, will you join the dance?
    Will you, won't you, will you, won't you, won't you join the dance?'

                                                                    L.C.

The Dong with a
Luminous Nose

When awful darkness and silence reign
Over the great Gromboolian plain,
   Through the long, long wintry nights; –
When the angry breakers roar
As they beat on the rocky shore; –
   When Storm-clouds brood on the towering heights
Of the Hills of the Chankly Bore: –

Then, through the vast and gloomy dark,
There moves what seems a fiery spark,
    A lonely spark with silvery rays
    Piercing the coal-black night, –
    A Meteor strange and bright: –
Hither and thither the vision strays,
    A single lurid light.

Slowly it wanders, – pauses, – creeps, –
Anon it sparkles, – flashes and leaps;
And ever as onward it gleaming goes
A light on the Bong-tree stems it throws.
And those who watch at that midnight hour
From Hall or Terrace, or lofty Tower,
Cry, as the wild light passes along, –
        'The Dong! – the Dong!
    The wandering Dong through the forest goes!
        The Dong! the Dong!
    The Dong with a luminous Nose!'

Long years ago
　　The Dong was happy and gay,
Till he fell in love with a Jumbly Girl
　　Who came to those shores one day,
For the Jumblies came in a sieve, they did, –
Landing at eve near the Zemmery Fidd
　　Where the Oblong Oysters grow,
　　And the rocks are smooth and grey.
And all the woods and the valleys rang
With the Chorus they daily and nightly sang, –
　　　'Far and few, far and few,
　　　Are the lands where the Jumblies live;
　　　Their heads are green, and their hands are blue
　　　And they went to sea in a sieve.'

Happily, happily passed those days!
　　While the cheerful Jumblies stayed;
　　They danced in circlets all night long,
　　To the plaintive pipe of the lively Dong,
　　　In moonlight, shine, or shade.
For day and night he was always there
By the side of the Jumbly Girl so fair,
With her sky-blue hands, and her sea-green hair.
Till the morning came of that hateful day
When the Jumblies sailed in their sieve away,
And the Dong was left on the cruel shore
Gazing – gazing for evermore, –
Ever keeping his weary eyes on
That pea-green sail on the far horizon, –
Singing the Jumbly Chorus still
As he sate all day on the grassy hill, –
　　　'Far and few, far and few,
　　　Are the lands where the Jumblies live;
　　　Their heads are green, and their hands are blue,
　　　And they went to sea in a sieve.'

But when the sun was low in the West,
    The Dong arose and said; –
'What little sense I once possessed
    Has quite gone out of my head!' –
And since that day he wanders still
By lake and forest, marsh and hill,
Singing – 'O somewhere, in valley or plain
Might I find my Jumbly Girl again!
For ever I'll seek by lake and shore
Till I find my Jumbly Girl once more!'

Playing a pipe with silvery squeaks,
Since then his Jumbly Girl he seeks,
And because by night he could not see,
He gathered the bark of the Twangum Tree
    On the flowery plain that grows.
    And he wove him a wondrous Nose, –
A Nose as strange as a Nose could be!
Of vast proportions and painted red,
And tied with cords to the back of his head.
        – In a hollow rounded space it ended
        With a luminous Lamp within suspended,
            All fenced about
            With a bandage stout
            To prevent the wind from blowing it out; –
And with holes all round to send the light,
In gleaming rays on the dismal night.

And now each night, and all night long,
Over those plains still roams the Dong;
And above the wail of the Chimp and Snipe
You may hear the squeak of his plaintive pipe
While ever he seeks, but seeks in vain
To meet with his Jumbly Girl again;
Lonely and wild – all night he goes, –
The Dong with a luminous Nose!
And all who watch at the midnight hour,
From Hall or Terrace, or lofty Tower,
Cry, as they trace the Meteor bright,
Moving along through the dreary night, –
        'This is the hour when forth he goes,
        The Dong with a luminous Nose!
        Yonder – over the plain he goes;
            He goes!
            He goes;
        The Dong with a luminous Nose!'

                                        E.L.

The Mad Hatter's Song

Twinkle, twinkle, little bat!
How I wonder what you're at!
Up above the world you fly,
Like a tea-tray in the sky.
                    Twinkle, twinkle –
                                    L.C.

The Quangle Wangle's Hat

I

On the top of the Crumpetty Tree
   The Quangle Wangle sat,
But his face you could not see,
   On account of his Beaver Hat.
For his Hat was a hundred and two feet wide,
With ribbons and bibbons on every side
And bells, and buttons, and loops and lace,
So that nobody ever could see the face
   Of the Quangle Wangle Quee.

II

The Quangle Wangle said
    To himself on the Crumpetty Tree, –
'Jam; and jelly; and bread;
    Are the best food for me!
But the longer I live on this Crumpetty Tree
The plainer than ever it seems to me
That very few people come this way
And that life on the whole is far from gay!'
      Said the Quangle Wangle Quee.

III

But there came to the Crumpetty Tree,
    Mr and Mrs Canary;
And they said, – 'Did you ever see
    Any spot so charmingly airy?
May we build a nest on your lovely Hat?
Mr Quangle Wangle, grant us that!
O please let us come and build a nest
Of whatever material suits you best,
      Mr Quangle Wangle Quee!'

IV

And besides, to the Crumpetty Tree
    Came the Stork, the Duck, and the Owl;
The Snail, and the Bumble-Bee,
    The Frog, and the Fimble Fowl;
(The Fimble Fowl, with a Corkscrew leg;)
And all of them said, – 'We humbly beg,
We may build our homes on your lovely Hat, –
Mr Quangle Wangle, grant us that!
      Mr Quangle Wangle Quee!'

V

And the Golden Grouse came there,
    And the Pobble who has no toes, –
And the small Olympian bear, –
    And the Dong with a luminous nose.
And the Blue Baboon, who played the flute, –
And the Orient Calf from the Land of Tute, –
And the Attery Squash, and the Bisky Bat, –
All came and built on the lovely Hat
    Of the Quangle Wangle Quee.

VI

And the Quangle Wangle said
    To himself on the Crumpetty Tree, –
'When all these creatures move
    What a wonderful noise there'll be!'
And at night by the light of the Mulberry moon
They danced to the Flute of the Blue Baboon,
On the broad green leaves of the Crumpetty Tree,
And all were as happy as happy could be,
    With the Quangle Wangle Quee.

E.L.

The King-Fisher Song

King Fisher courted Lady Bird –
Sing Beans, sing Bones, sing Butterflies!
  'Find me my match,' he said,
  'With such a noble head –
With such a beard, as white as curd –
  With such expressive eyes!'

'Yet pins have heads,' said Lady Bird –
Sing Prunes, sing Prawns, sing Primrose-Hill!
  'And, where you stick them in,
  They stay, and thus a pin
Is very much to be preferred
  To one that's never still!'

'Oysters have beards,' said Lady Bird –
Sing Flies, sing Frogs, sing Fiddle-strings!
   'I love them, for I know
   They never chatter so:
They would not say one single word –
   Not if you crowned them Kings!'

'Needles have eyes,' said Lady Bird –
Sing Cats, sing Corks, sing Cowslip-tea!
   'And they are sharp – just what
   Your Majesty is *not*:
So get you gone – 'tis too absurd
   To come a-courting *me*!'

                    L.C.

The Pelican Chorus

King and Queen of the Pelicans we;
No other Birds so grand we see!
None but we have feet like fins!
With lovely leathery throats and chins!

Ploffskin, Pluffskin, Pelican jee!
We think no Birds so happy as we!
Plumpskin, Ploshkin, Pelican jill!
We think so then, and we thought so still!

We live on the Nile. The Nile we love.
By night we sleep on the cliffs above;
By day we fish, and at eve we stand
On long bare islands of yellow sand.
And when the sun sinks slowly down
And the great rock walls grow dark and brown,
Where the purple river rolls fast and dim
And the Ivory Ibis starlike skim,
Wing to wing we dance around, –
Stamping our feet with a flumpy sound, –
Opening our mouths as Pelicans ought,
And this is the song we nightly snort; –

Ploffskin, Pluffskin, Pelican jee!
We think no Birds so happy as we!
Plumpskin, Ploshkin, Pelican jill!
We think so then, and we thought so still!

Last year came out our Daughter, Dell;
And all the Birds received her well.
To do her honour, a feast we made
For every bird that can swim or wade.
Herons and Gulls, and Cormorants black,
Cranes, and Flamingoes with scarlet back,
Plovers and Storks, and Geese in clouds,
Swans and Dilberry Ducks in crowds.
Thousands of Birds in wondrous flight!
They ate and drank and danced all night,
And echoing back from the rocks you heard
Multitude-echoes from Bird and Bird, –

    Ploffskin, Pluffskin, Pelican jee!
    We think no Birds so happy as we!
    Plumpskin, Ploshkin, Pelican jill!
    We think so then, and we thought so still!

Yes, they came; and among the rest,
The King of the Cranes all grandly dressed.
Such a lovely tail! Its feathers float
Between the ends of his blue dress-coat;
With pea-green trousers all so neat,
And a delicate frill to hide his feet, –
(For though no one speaks of it, every one knows,
He has got no webs between his toes!)

As soon as he saw our Daughter Dell,
In violent love that Crane King fell, –
On seeing her waddling form so fair,
With a wreath of shrimps in her short white hair.
And before the end of the next long day,
Our Dell had given her heart away;
For the King of the Cranes had won that heart,
With a Crocodile's egg and a large fish-tart.
She vowed to marry the King of the Cranes,
Leaving the Nile for stranger plains;
And away they flew in a gathering crowd
Of endless birds in a lengthening cloud.

Ploffskin, Pluffskin, Pelican jee!
We think no Birds so happy as we!
Plumpskin, Ploshkin, Pelican jill!
We think so then, and we thought so still!

And far away in the twilight sky,
We heard them singing a lessening cry, –
Farther and farther till out of sight,
And we stood alone in the silent night!
Often since, in the nights of June,
We sit on the sand and watch the moon; –
She has gone to the great Gromboolian plain,
And we probably never shall meet again!
Oft, in the long still nights of June,
We sit on the rocks and watch the moon; –
She dwells by the streams of the Chankly Bore,
And we probably never shall see her more.

Ploffskin, Pluffskin, Pelican jee!
We think no Birds so happy as we!
Plumpskin, Ploshkin, Pelican jill!
We think so then, and we thought so still!

E.L.

The Red Queen's Lullaby

Hush-a-by lady, in Alice's lap!
Till the feast's ready, we've time for a nap:
When the feast's over, we'll go to the ball –
Red Queen, and White Queen, and Alice, and all!

L.C.

Index of Titles and First Lines

First lines are in italics

Notes on the Authors

EDWARD LEAR 1812–1888

Edward Lear was born in Holloway, London, the twentieth child of a stockbroker. His childhood was an unhappy one, and throughout his life he suffered from epilepsy and depression. Lear first attracted attention by his paintings of birds, and later turned to landscapes. Through his work as a zoological draughtsman he came under the patronage of the Earl of Derby, and it was for the Earl's grand-children that he wrote *A Book of Nonsense* (1846), with his own limericks and illustrations. Later nonsense volumes included *Nonsense Songs, Stories, Botany and Alphabets* (1870), which contains 'The Owl and the Pussy-cat' and 'The Jumblies'; and *Laughable Lyrics* (1876). Lear travelled widely, in Italy, Greece, Egypt, and India, publishing books on his travels with his own illustrations. In 1870 he settled in San Remo, where he lived until his death.

LEWIS CARROLL 1832–1898

Lewis Carroll was the pen name of Charles Lutwidge Dodgson. Born in Daresbury, Cheshire, he was educated at Rugby and Christ Church, Oxford, where he became a lecturer in Mathematics in 1855. His most famous work, *Alice's Adventures in Wonderland* (1865) originated in a boat trip with the young daughters of H. G. Liddell, the Dean of Christ Church: Lorina, Alice, and Edith. It was for Alice that he expanded his impromptu story into book form, giving her the manuscript, then called 'Alice's Adventures Underground', as a Christmas present in 1864. Another book of adventures followed, *Through the Looking-Glass, and What Alice Found There* (1871). These two 'Alice' books, both illustrated by John Tenniel, contain many of Lewis Carroll's famous poems. Other works include the mock heroic nonsense poem, 'The Hunting of the Snark' (1876), and *Sylvie and Bruno*. He also published mathematics books under his own name and was among the pioneers of portrait photography.

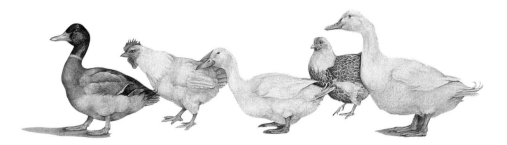